© 2016 Pia Mookland

All Rights Reserved

PLAID

With love for Elaine, for without her constant wisdom and support over many years, this book would not be possible. I have tremendous gratitude for Sun, Moon and anyone who helped me along the way. A wise woman once told me "friends are family we choose." ♡

Note to A Reader

This book was written in both English and American Sign Language or ASL. ASL, the language of the deaf has it's own rules that differ from English. Hearing readers may find noticeable differences in vocabulary, punctuation and word order. These are intentional on my part.

Doctor's Notes

This is the case of a three month old child who is suffering from malnutrition, said to be vomiting repeatedly, has been brought to the hospital and given good nursing care.

and good diet. She recovered very well. She gained weight and because the mother is deaf and dumb, she was given some specific instructions and it was asked that the neighbors and relatives help in the care of this child.

Date of Admit: July 29, 1968

Date of Discharge: August 9, 1968

Diagnosis: Malnutrition

— Dr. Silliker

Deaf and dumb is an archaic term used to describe deaf people who cannot use their voices to speak and is considered offensive in deaf culture by todays standards.

Doctor's Notes
September 1992

I am writing in regards to our mutual client who I have been working with for the past several months in my capacity as a clinical specialist.

Our client is an intelligent young woman who sought therapy in order to deal with her history of severe ritual abuse which was ongoing for many years. While she is clearly a survivor with many strengths, the traumatic effects of the abuse on her life have been profound... seriously impacting on the development of her potential, interfering with her capacity to feel safe in the world, and compromising her ability to have meaningful relationships in which she can develop a sense of trust with another person. It has taken a great deal of courage for her to seek therapy which will undoubtedly involve a long process of healing given the severity and extent of the abuse. She definitely needs as much support as she can get, emotional as well as financial as her resources are limited. If I can be of further assistance in advocating for this rather remarkable woman I would be more than happy to do so. - Clinical Nurse Specialist

Letter from a Lawyer

As you know the grand jury handed down the following indictments on May 10, 1991. There is currently a superior court warrant outstanding. The warrant number is 886892. The indictments are as follows:

Rape of a child under 16 years with force – 10 counts

Rape of a child under 16 years with force – 10 counts:

Unnatural rape of a child with force under the age of 16 – 10 counts

Indecent assault and battery on a child - 10 counts
Indecent assault and battery on a child under 14 years 10 more counts.
Thank you for your testimony and co-operation.

I know it wasn't easy to testify before the Grand Jury but you did very well and thus the indictments issued. Please call if you have questions. Have a wonderful summer. I will be in touch if he is arrested or we receive any news of his whereabouts. - Assistant D.A. Chief Child Abuse Unit. In case you were wondering about the charge that was outstanding the end results was 10 more counts.

This makes a total of 60 counts or charges of rape. Do not be fooled. There were way more rapes than those counted by the court system. These indictments were indicative of the more "memorable" events that could be testified about in a court of law. Do not be fooled by legal terminology that uses terms like indecent or unnatural. No rapes are decent or natural. The terms are used to classify rapes.

A cleaner way to explain things. I think it would be better to label things more clearly for a society in denial. Things like rape of a six year old, rape of a nine year old. By using the terms under the age of 14 or under the age of 16

It does not allow the full impact of what occurs in the life of a sexually abused child to enter the lay person's mind but this is how the legal system does things to create various levels of crimes. I told myself I was not going to censure myself

In my writings, readers, I encourage you to stay on and learn if you can but also do what you need to do in order to take care of yourself. It's not a pretty reality. Some people don't want to believe sexual abuse

Happens to infants, toddlers, kindergarden age kids, grade school kids and high schoolers. I am here to tell you, it does. Here is some first-hand knowledge and experiences from my malnourished life.

Let's first understand the term "UNNATURAL RAPE". It includes oral contact between the mouth of one person and the penis of another. Penis, oral, contact of one persons mouth on the vagina, vulva or labia of another person, masturbation of another person or any intrusion of a part of one's person's body or some other object into the genital or anal opening of another person's body. The offender committed these acts intentionally, and thirdly that the sexual act was done in a public place

Where the defendent either intends public exposure or has reckless disregard for a substantial risk of public exposure. Indecent assault means touching any part of the anatomy thought private such as a person's genital area or buttocks or the breasts of females.

if the child is under the age of 14 it is irrelevant whether or not there was consent. For the record, I never gave consent at the age of a pre-schooler, a grade schooler, a high schooler or legal adult at the age of 18. But more about that comes later.

Rape of a child in my state is defined as whoever unlawfully has sexual intercourse or unnatural conduct with a child under the age of 16. Remember how they pretty it up by making one think of a 16 year old. But think infant, toddler, pre-schooler, grade schooler, high schooler.

After discharge from the hospital at 4 months old, my "deaf and dumb" mother makes arrangements somehow for me to live with my grandparents... She left my father some time after this and we all lived on the first floor of a family home. My maternal grandparents

living upstairs. From
what I've been told
and in scarce pictures
I gained weight from
4 months to 1 year when
I lived with my grandparents.
To hear my mother tell it
I just wouldn't eat. I
couldn't keep food down.
My deaf and dumb

father did not give my mother money for food. My father was said to be a drinker and a batterer and was not really a big presence in my life. to hear my father tell it my mother "prevented him from court ordered visitation."

From my 6 year old perspective both of them blamed and bad-mouthed the other. I waited at the window the first Saturdays of the month and very often he didn't show. He would also come when not allowed and she didn't let him see us.

By us, I mean my oldest sister hearing and my younger deaf. This was how we would be introduced. This is so and so, she is hearing. This is so and so she is deaf. I would watch the reaction of the person as to the favorability of being hearing.

Now one can read lots about Deaf culture if one wishes. There's big "D" in Deaf and little "d" in deaf depending on one's personal views. What was hard for me sometimes was determining what was deafness and what was just plain dysfunctional living and what was intertwined. Back in the day, disabled people were hidden at home uneducated. My mother deaf did not go to school until age 12 or so and quit at the age of 16. Laments of "woe is me those stupid hearing

People" a frequent topic of Saturday conversation sandwiched between the words to me "I only wanted one child" and "you are a devil child" "a black hearted girl." False allegations and violent accusations. "You didn't tell everything that was said did you?" "Stupid Hearing People".

Relentless repetitive conversation. My mother deaf says we children were her punishment. She knows nothing of me then or now. I knew in first grade my mother didn't understand my homework. In her case, she was not smarter than a six year old.

But she did know enough to hide certain behaviors. It's odd to be someone's ears all the time while trying to figure out what it is you do not know and how to translate so one is not called a stupid hearing person like the other ignorant people of the times.

All the while knowing my mother deaf was wrong. Most people hearing wanted to do their best to communicate but in some instances just unaware of what deaf people's challenges were. My mother deaf didn't realize I straddled both hearing and deaf worlds. Daily fixing her broken

English, changing what hearing people said to help my mother deaf understand. I resided in both worlds. Living a noisy existence. Everyday filtering noises, potential threats, scary thoughts of who protects me from a burglar. One memory I have is of the emergency room when I was about five is not being protected from the doctor putting a sheet over my head. I said to the doctor "I am not dead yet." Guess I saw too much television where the face is covered by the doctor with a sheet and the tag is placed on the dead person's toe. Turns out I had to translate to myself that "all would be okay" it's just a cloth to get a clean area when getting 3 stitches "for my face". It will be okay. It will only pinch and I will not die and the doctor knows "I am not dead." Soldier on......

Letter From My Inner Soldier

Your license to parent has been revoked when you launch your attacks unprovoked. Hacking at my ankles with the laundry stick. Leaving red welts and splintered nicks. Increasingly familiar with patterns ingrained in the wood,

From morning to night in the corner I stood. Not moving a muscle was no easy task. But for fear of my mother I did as she asked. Allowed to toilet but once per day after this I was back in the corner to stay.

Daring to ask twice
meant expecting the worst.
So I held my bladder 'til
I thought it would burst.
I was not to shift weight
from one foot to the other
or I'd face the wrath of
my dear mother. I was
to remain in absolute
silence or become once
again a victim of violence

Fortunately mother couldn't see inside me. My imagination allowed to roam free making piles of creative ways to pass the time mentally reading stories or nursery rhymes. This took my mind off the pain in my feet, the ache in my arms, the wish for a seat. This would work for a very short while then I'd reach up again to the top of the pile. Just when I thought I'd go completely numb, the moon had come out and bedtime had come. Some of the insane reasons for earning corner time included eating sugar from the sugar bowl, making scratches on the fridge, and most of all spitting on my brother and causing a teething rash on his chin. All ludicrous accusations of course. Perhaps now is a good time to introduce baby number 4 - boy - hearing

GOLDEN CHILD. He was followed shortly by twin girls. Deaf. One of my earliest memories is seeing the two of them side by side in a matching pair of bassinets. Their heads tilted at opposite angles, I looked and knew they were different.

Excerpts from a Neurologist Consultation 1977

Chief complaint: Questionable seizure activity. The 4 and a half year old patient continues in her present special program for the hearing impaired where she continues to have a lot of purposeless movement and self-stimulating behavior which was not responsive to anti-convulsant medication. Her instructor feels that she is making significant improvement, making eye contact more frequently and following instructions somewhat better. She is in a program with her twin sister. The instructor feels that the two girls have entirely different personalities and feels the other twin is a normal child aside from her hearing loss. She does not exhibit any of the extraneous movements. Examination today was quite difficult as the patient was quite anxious and fearful.

She would not co-operate with developmental testing. Although she has shown improvement, she is clearly not responding to medication. EEG was normal but this does not rule out a seizure disorder. Her teacher who comes with her today is quite concerned about her behavior. She is very hyperactive and involved in a great deal of self-stimulatory behavior. She is unable to communicate with people or make her needs known without gross gestures. She frequently stares up at lights and makes loud purposeless noises.

Her twin's behavior is not unlike her own. They are both involved in behavior modification class at the school for the deaf. Her instructor is also concerned with the presence of spells lasting seconds in which her eyes will stare and eyelids will flutter. She then resumes normal play activity. This exam reveals an active girl who makes loud noises with frequent teeth grinding and seemingly oblivious to her surroundings. Pupils reactive to light. She has two colors in each eye.

Her twin has one blue eye and one brown eye. Impression: Waardenberg Syndrome; developmental delay, great deal of self-stimulating and autistic-like behavior. While she has shown improvement since last being seen, she is not responding to medication and the major difficulty is that she does not generalize the behavior she has in school to the home situation. Mother is anxious to find residential placement for both twins but the wait at the preferred placement is quite considerable.

No scheduled follow-up is needed at this time.
— Dr. Singer

Now looking back their instructor was correct in suggesting motor seizures on occasion. Autism is now definite. She was incorrect in suggesting her twin was a normal child. She also has autism and developmental delay. Dr. Singer states that the patient is seemingly oblivious to her surroundings. This is only partially true. They with their two color eyes saw our lives at home. Their two colored eyes saw our mother go to hit them for purposeless movement. They learned to walk fast to avoid her whenever possible. They did not have to endure looking at patterns ingrained in wooden corners. But they did have to look at the same thing in the living room. All day. Every day.

I believe the reason they did not generalize the behavior learned at school was mostly out of fear. Who would they be today with the early intervention they got had they not had fear? That will never be known. They saw the same 1970's green plaid

Sofa and brown paneled walls. Not allowed freedom of movement or to get up from the seat. Hyperactive teeth grinding girls. They learned they'd be hit. Not oblivious to their surroundings. What they saw happen to us and what they felt now or then will never be known.

They are unable to discuss feelings or things not in the here and now. They sat. They each had their spot on the couch green plaid. On good days, they had us. A buffer when we were not in the corner. They had my ears. When my mother headed their way

I WOULD WARN them to stop their MOVEMENTS AND Self-Stimulatory Behaviors. On BAD DAYS, it WAS BAD for ALL of US ALL AROUND. Their Respective PLAID Couch Cushions Pressed flat. The MIDDLE Cushion PLUMP. OLDER Sister Hearing, ME AND YOUNGER Sister DEAF

Were to sit on the floor to keep the furniture "good". I KNOW YOU ARE PROBABLY WONDERING ABOUT WHERE THE FATHER OF THE LAST THREE KIDS IS AND I GUESS I CAN STALL NO LONGER.

I do not know when my mother and the father of Golden Boy Hearing and Twins deaf met, but from years of birth I was around the age of two. I do not remember exactly when he moved in, but do remember us kids wondering who he was and hoping he'd stay as our mother was much happier and less focused on us. For all intents and purposes, he became the male figure head in our lives given the absence of my father. Our financial situation had improved. We did lots more recreational things.

We were allowed more freedoms but Mother deaf was still very emotionally cold. She offered no affection. No compliments. No attention. No encouragement to develop a sense of self. She offered no delight in me. No interest in my thoughts, likes and dislikes, and most of all my feelings. I learned quickly to keep opinions and feelings to myself. They were not discussed and if anger reared its head, you were shamed into submission. My stepfather Deaf was a bit different. He offered affection, compliments and a feeling of being protected for the first time in my life. Little did I know, he was beginning a grooming process. He found a needy vulnerable woman with an instant family of girls who were love starved. He varied his techniques according to the situation.

One technique involved gaining trust. Frequently at night, while mother deaf was asleep, he'd wake me up to ask me how my feet felt after standing all day. He pretended to care and said "I will try with your mother tomorrow to see if you can get out of the corner and be allowed to play outside." He made me feel at times that He was powerless against Mother deaf too. He'd say "Don't tell Mother we spoke tonight or she will get mad and not let you outside." Sometimes He made me think His plan worked and I got to play outside. I

He gave me compliments telling me that "I am a big girl" and that "I am good." Lifting my face to his while telling me "I am a pretty girl." This is a tactic called secrecy. Isolating me further from my mother deaf who calls me a "devil black-hearted" child who lies all the time". Not translating "All ll" the words. Keeping Secrets from Her. Now I really have kept things from her. This tactic is called Collusion. A Sharing of Secrets. There is also an element of alienating me from my siblings by seemingly being the preferred child.

This tactic is called isolation. I don't remember a lot of specifics of how the first "incident" took place, but have inklings that Mother deaf had hit me a lot that day. Beat me. Stepfather deaf got me up at night and seated me on his lap while I cried. He would hug me and tell me "I was a good girl" and that "Mother dear was wrong about me." I wore a white pajama set with green piping. He usually sat in his worn out pale boxers. He'd hug me and soothe me. Lift up my face tell me "I'm pretty" and then ask to see both my face and for a "look in my underwear." I remember feeling alarmed and confused. Just "a quick look at my pretty vagina" me gripping my elastic waistband tightly close to my body. That may have been it the first time while he waited to see if I kept the secret. This tactic is called desensitization and using fear that he could stop helping me with mother deaf and withdraw his "affection." Another way I was made "complicit" was being the "ears" to listen for my mother deaf

to wake up on nights
my step-father deaf
"comforted" me. Those many nights.
I should also tell you
another way he tried
to gain trust. He told me
that my bedroom wall
that connected to my mothers
room had a small peephole.
The peephole was very

important information for my safety. I neglected to mention earlier that in addition to controlling my body movements during the day in the corner, Mother deaf also controlled how I slept. Mother deaf had a specific position in which I was to sleep.

if she found me in my bed in the wrong position I would be hit awake. The correct sleeping position consisted of laying on your stomach, face to the wall, legs together, arms outstretched towards the edges of the mattress. I called this position the Jesus Christ position.

"God sees you" she'd say. There was a large crucifix on the peephole wall. She chose this sleep position because she didn't want me to "pull on my tits to make them grow." Despite Jesus' crucifix watching me, I "relaxed" in my bed on guard listening for my

Mother deaf's slippers heading toward her bedroom. I would then assume the "correct sleeping position." However, I couldn't remain awake and on guard all the time. In my sleep I would naturally move positions and awake to a wide selection of items.

Such spanking instruments included a wooden hand that didn't hurt much and didn't get used a lot, the laundry stick which was an orange broken broom handle made of wood that was used to push cloth diapers around in the washing machine, the "strap"

A red leather dog leash with chain on the end, and a taped 1.5 inch wide stick that looked like a longish ruler. This was called the "Heat of the Seat." It was bought on a family vacation in Pennsylvania Dutch Country specifically for the purposes of spanking. The little girl on the end of the stick had

A red butt depicted much like myself. I remember wondering is this okay behavior? Since it is sold does everyone get hit? Older sister Hearing and I took a chance and buried the red "strap" inside an empty CoolWhip container in a neighbor's yard when mother deaf and step-father

Deaf took a solo vacation leaving us with Auntie. We figured the beating we got for the missing spanking tool would be well worth getting rid of the most painful tool. We were never accused. However, the strap was replaced with step-father Deaf's leather belt with a big metal buckle depicting a brown horse design. There was also no bullying Mother deaf's hands and fists. My first grade teacher, the only teacher to question anything in my life, kept me next to her desk the entire day because I wouldn't tell her what really happened to my upper arm. I had 5 fingernail marks/scabs but I told her my cat did it.

Second and third grade are a miserable blur. Repression: a psychic numbing or blocking out of memory or feeling of a trauma. Just so you know, I tried to locate the peephole but never did.

Some might wonder why I didn't say anything or blame the victim. Beside feeling fear and shame, I didn't trust adults. I had already been let down too much by my own family. My relatives who lived above us, who asked what was all that racket last night and did nothing.

Teachers who did nothing but say "I am not living up to my potential." Neighbors who never saw any friends over our house. People who noticed marks on my arms or my dirty disheveled appearance who all said nothing. Our shuttered-closed-dark curtained house was where I invisibly existed. My mother deaf, aside from her physical abuse and her emotional neglect, showed me that she could not be a trusted adult by her inaction when I ran into a situation with a neighbor. My older sister Hearing and I were playing Hide and Seek and the neighbor's house was open. My older sister Hearing said we ran around in that house alot, but I only remember that one time. I remember my neighbor as a mostly bedridden man with 1 and ½ legs. I remember he spent a lot of time on his bed. His living-room/bed faced our backdoor. He spent a lot of time on his bed with the door to the outside open. As a child, I remember wondering about that but figured he couldn't get around again or go outside. As an adult, I wonder if it wasn't for a more sinister reason. I counted, while older sister Hearing hid somewhere upstairs. He tells me to "come over to see my stump." I remember feeling odd but also curious about what was under his bandages. It's all I remember of that. Older

Sister Hearing tells me I was very mad at her for not coming when I called her over and over. After this, I returned to my own yard where lots of my aunts and uncles were gathered. It must have been a holiday since my relatives were over. Mother deaf couldn't very well keep us indoors while she spent time outdoors. Everyone seated in their lawn chairs sporadically speaking French inside a wide circle. At least a dozen people with their spouses this hot summer day. When I looked around at their faces I knew

Something was wrong but I did not know what. I must have told them about the neighbor showing me his "stump" as the circle went quiet. I did not understand as "Home Signs" were being used to talk to my mother. A "Home Sign" is sign language that is unique between two people or a family at home when one or more people do not know how to sign. Basically one makes up their own sign and my mother deaf had understood it from childhood. None of my aunts or uncles knew sign language as it was forbidden to use at the time.

My mother deaf angrily told me not to play over there again. Everyone was still quiet and tense. I got really afraid. I asked "Am I going to grow one of those on my thigh?" I began to cry hard. Everyone said "No" but they were of no comfort to me.

The only one to comfort me was Auntie's boyfriend. No one else was saying a word. He held me and reassured me I was okay and wouldn't be growing anything. I had never been hugged like that before. I remember thinking something bad happened and no one would be explaining it to me. Looking back it was a prime time for some safety skills training. It set the tone for further victimization. In first grade, the boy who sat in front of me turned around in his seat in the middle of class. He took his penis out of his zipper and showed me. I remember thinking is this normal? Is it something about me? Why does this happen to me? In fourth grade I had to change schools. "I needed discipline." I didn't know why and hadn't been to the principal's office. I was changing from public to private parochial school, even though we weren't church-going practicing Catholics. I didn't see why I had to go but now looking back, perhaps it was a way to further isolate and alienate me from my siblings. I wore

A maroon plaid jumper and white shirt with a Peter Pan collar. I was grateful for a school uniform because clothes in school were becoming more of an issue in determining coolness and I wasn't going to be it with the clothes I had.

I wouldn't have been able to remain invisible. I'd be a target for bullies. I could only bathe or wash my hair once a week but puberty and greasy hair and skin go hand in hand. I got my period at age 9 before transferring to this new school.

I was at the Hilltop Steakhouse on July 4, 1976 the Bicentennial. I wore a red shirt, blue pants with a white rope tie at the waist. I thought I was dying. Next thing I remember is Mother deaf handing me a pad in the bathroom. She said "Now you can get pregnant."

She later said to me, "I think you will be pregnant by the age of 16." This was the extent of my sex education. She said this quite often. In looking back, I don't know why she thought this since I never left the house. At the time, I did think that

Kissing had something to do with pregnancy because my mother deaf always changed the tv channel when a kissing scene came on. I thought boys had something special in their Adams apple since their voices changed into men. I had a best school only friend who straightened me out with Judy Blume's book *Are You There God? It's Me Margaret*. Mother deaf found and confiscated it when she looked inside and saw the word... period. It was a library book and she wasn't going to give it back until she read it. We all know she probably reads

At a first grade level and my friend probably hasn't gotten it back yet. Mother dear forbade us to read books so I'd sneak them home in my underwear. Luckily, in school the book mobile would come. I would read by the light of the moonlight made by a crack in the window shade and reflected onto the wall a small sliver of light. I read and listened for my mother deaf's slippered footsteps. That all changed in my new school. No more book mobile. Perhaps I was sent alone to another school so I'd be more accessible. Stepfather deaf worked the night shift and would be leaving work as I walked to school. He would take this opportunity to divert me from walking to school. Somedays I would just miss homeroom. Some days, I'd be out half-a-day. Other days a full day. He would write my excuse notes. Teachers accepted them. I sometimes felt teachers didn't make more of an effort to communicate due to the deafness and felt too much sympathy for them than they did my well-being. Other times, I felt they had suspected abuse of some kind but did nothing. One place stepfather deaf took me when he diverted me from school was about 20 minutes drive. We would pass the sign that read "if you lived here you'd be home now" and arrive at the home of friend deaf's light green double decker. Step-father deaf had his own key but he only used it during school hours.

His friend Deaf worked day shift. A perfect arrangement for step-father Deaf. After step-father Deaf did his "Business", he would nap asking me to wake him by a certain time. Always in time to be dropped off on my walk home from school. Route me in my Catholic school jumper uniform blending in with the sea of maroon plaid other children. Where Mother deaf thought he was I'll never know. What his friend deaf thought he was using his home for I'll never know. Another purpose of this home was to show me some

Magazines I had never seen before. I didn't understand why the children had black boxes over their heads and eyes. I equated the black boxes with the blindfolds he would place on me. He would pose me or tell me to do what the kids are doing in the pictures.

I DO NOT REMEMBER if POLOROIDS WERE TAKEN BUT I REMEMBER the SOUNDS. I WOULDN'T DOUBT it. I REMEMBER THINKING I HOPE I DON'T APPEAR AS ONE OF THESE BLACK BOX CHILDREN. NAKED CHILDREN IN A MAGAZINE. CERTAINLY, HE HAD HIS OWN PRIVATE COLLECTION OF PHOTOS.

My maroon plaid uniform collapsed in a heap in friend deaf's "if you lived here you'd be home now" living room. The running joke was that this friend deaf couldn't ever find a girlfriend. A butt of jokes weak man who took all kinds of abuse from step-father deaf.

I hope friend deaf did not willingly or knowingly allow his home to be used this way as I rather liked and felt for friend deaf. Was he complicit in step-father deaf's schemes to further shame or abuse me? Was he in on the plan to take my virginity?

Recollections of a Jingle

Twice the lather. You'll be a little lovelier each day. With fabulous pink Camay. The soap for beautiful women. This is at least what I told myself unconvincingly in the "if you lived here you'd be home now" house.

Ordered to take a shower at friend deaf's house. Events jumbled in my mind. Lying on the living room floor in a pile like discarded clothing refusing to move. Not caring to ever get up.

Furniture moved arms bound get up! get up! Stepfather says "Take a shower!

I stood in the water. I reach for the soap. Camay. Pink. Blood and lather sliding down my legs. A pink water swirling at my feet. Circling then washing me away down the drain. It seemed like it would never stop. The soap for beautiful women I told myself.

You'll be a little lovelier each day with fabulous Pink Camay. Shower to Shower each day helps keep odor away when you Shower to Shower each day. I remember no more before or after this shower. Twice the lather twice the lather

This plaid maroon jumper I wore grade 4 through 6 served as a daily reminder of my shame. It traveled with me to many experiences. The nuns saw fit to change our uniforms in grade seven to a less form fitting plaid maroon skirt, Peter Pan shirt.

and matching vests to cover budding breasts. My jumper plaid walked me home one day. Upon arrival, I pushed the door but it was locked. Naturally my parents deaf couldn't hear I was home. So I did what I usually did at these most frustrating times. Not wanting to get in trouble for not coming straight home from school. I banged on the door. I strained my ears to hear where in the house they might be. I waved flat paper under the door. I circled the house jumping up to touch windows only to sit down and wait. I wanted to scream. "Don't you know I come home everyday at this time?" Why am I not good enough to have a key?" As luck would have it, I really had to pee. My house's entryway shared a common hallway with my maternal

Grandfather and Auntie hearing. Despite not having much contact with upstairs, I risked asking to use the bathroom. To this day a full bladder and no bathroom makes me very angry. Auntie at work, I struggled to ask my

French speaking grandfather if I could use the bathroom. He thumped his walker all the way back to the only chair old I ever saw him in after he had let me in. After I use the toilet, I begin my exit downstairs he beckons me over.

He is old and I do as I'm told. He pulls me onto his lap holding me there. Me and my Catholic jumper. He makes me watch TV. General Hospital. With him as I smell old people smell mixed with wintergreen. He mutters in French.

Then struggles in English
points to my uniform
and asks if I go to church
on Sundays. I really don't
answer since we aren't
really Catholic. He laughs
as Luke and Laura kiss.
His Indian corn teeth
exposed. He grips me

tighter and shows me some white wiry hairs from his pulled down zipper. I was initially afraid of hurting him, then very surprised by the strength in him. At the sight of his shriveled penis, I forced myself off his lap while he laughed through rotted teeth and dry mouth. As I go to leave he says "bye" and calls me by my mother dear's name. I ponder this knowing from now on to hold my pee. I should tell you that some thirty years later the plaid maroon jumper is still with me. As if each memory is stored in separate maroon squares bored into it by my stare. Perhaps I shall now update you on things downstairs. Most everyone is in different schools. The twins now placed in a residential school only to return to the couch green plaid on weekends, holidays and school vacations. Since six children share one peephole bedroom, the Jesus Christ sleep position had to be eliminated. Our breasts grown in. The twins sharing a twin bunk bed with sisters hearing. Corner time also faded away with the last beating I got. Mother Leaf held me upside down by the feet while hitting me. My head and neck bending unnaturally on the floor. Fear of a broken neck made me for the first and last time Hit Mother deaf Back. I got my foot free and kicked the only spot available to Mt. Stomach. Earning corner time But well worth it. She knew she could not control me physically anymore. But for fear of foster Homes and Being split up kept me quiet. Back then my fear was there was no place for deaf, mentally retarded, autistic twins with behavioral and sleep challenges. If there were such a place would they take them both? Would they be safe there with

No way to communicate to people who didn't know their gestures? I was really, really stuck. Gripping fear to keep silent my constant shadow. Isolation from the outside world a constant except for school. All my conversations monitored. The ones siblings hearing

And Deaf did have with me were met with unsatisfying results. No one would talk about life in our home. Everyone employing their own coping strategy that worked for them. Sexual abuse was not discussed. Ever. Much like any feelings, thoughts or emotions. Truthtellers aren't popular.

Stepfather deaf remained in our home while she became more and more unhappy with him. She would question him as to why he locked her into her bedroom at night as he sat with a dumb stare not answering. Other times, I had seen Mother deaf tell Stepfather deaf to go sleep in my bed during the day. She allowed him to take me on solo trips to the store, deaf clubs and out of state to visit his family. She allowed him even after arguments about why he could not take my other siblings along with me.

She knew what was going on no question. She acted jealous and resentful towards me. I remember feeling confused about her thinking that there was some kind of subtle competition between us but there wasn't on my end.

One example is very vivid in my mind. Forgive me for jumping ahead in time but clearly demonstrates Mother deaf participating in or allowing certain behaviors. Step-father deaf stood Mother deaf and me next to each other by the kitchen sink as he sat across from us in his usual chair Brown

He said "look" "compare" "Who has the better breasts?" I stood in utter silence and disbelief. Mother deaf in a blue Izod stood there for the "competition" and was upset to be declared the loser. He "looked" "compared" and took a photo of us. Mother deaf did

Nothing but get angry at me. I was about 14 years old. Life had not changed much and there seemed to me to be no way out of it. My own mother dear was not going to be there for me, ever. How could she allow this behavior? How could he be so bold as to do this?

What kind of life is this? It seemed never-ending. All this suffering for what? Where is this God I am learning about in my Catholic jumper plaid maroon? One day when I was nine, I thought I was about to find out when I drowned at the beach. I had been floating on a tire and was sucked out to sea. I came off the tire not knowing how to swim. Panic set in for I knew the beach had been nearly empty. My family non-swimmers.

My short life flashed before my eyes. I thought about my family. What kind of abuse would my sisters twins endure without me to protect them? I thought about what it would be like for all present to go home to my mother deaf with one less sibling? Would my mother deaf even grieve for me?

She had never expressed affection towards me. I would die without her ever telling me she loved me even when I asked her point blank, but that's a different story. Belief flooded all these thoughts and more as a kind of spiritual presence(s) had convinced me to let

My present day life worries and stresses go so we could move forward. I then was flooded with questions. Why are we here on earth? What am I supposed to do in this life? What religion is the right one? How did the world come to be? This was only the beginning.

They answered only some of my questions reassuring me answers in due time. I cannot even begin to describe the sense of peace, comfort, and pure love, I felt for the first time in my life and nothing since. In my present life, has come close to that feeling. The spiritual presence showed me instances from my 9 year life span. It was not what was occurring but what I felt about what I saw that seemed important. We had a dialogue about aspects of the future and I thought I made a wrong choice when they told me I must go back. They didn't force me. it would have to be my decision. They gently prodded me into going. Once I relented, the difference was very overwhelming. I did not want to leave this loving place only to return to my miserable life on earth. I had argued and pleaded. They told me my mission in life was not over. I had to sadly give up and return to my earthly body. Arms grabbed me about the waist pulling me hard to shore while I slammed back into my body. I felt the cold again. The salt stinging my throat.

I WAS DEPOSITED ON the FAMILY BLANKET MY toes touching SAND. I did NOT THANK MY RESCUER AS I WAS Still quite STUNNED BY MY EXPERIENCE. NEGLECT ONCE MORE INVADED MY Life. INSTEAD OF GOING TO THE HOSPITAL, STEP-FATHER DEAF COLLECTED CHILDREN HEARING AND DEAF LOADED UP

Station Wagon Blue and headed for home. With the spirits looking out for me, I had to stop the car on the way home to vomit tons and tons of water. All the while, I thought about our purpose in life. Our purpose in life is to just love.

It is hard to imagine loving people that hurt me and then having to go back for more. But go back I did. I must share one more story of the jumper maroon plaid before retiring it for the maroon skirt plaid and conservative vest of grade seven

And eight. One day after school, (this was a change, and experience told me this change is never good) step-father deaf picked me up at school in the station wagon blue. He takes me to the parking lot of a grocery store. This store always confused me. It was both heartland and purity supreme. I had no idea what dangers to expect from a supermarket. I was however quite familiar with the dangers that lurked in the station wagon blue with the drop down trunk that doubled as a cot

For travel weary step-fathers on crowded camping trips and family vacations. This time was different. I was left alone inside the car trying to figure out whats coming next. Step-father Deaf entered Heartland Purity Supreme Take your pick.

My mind racing knowing something bad would be coming next. Perhaps our next destination. I mean what harm can come from a store that sells groceries? I had no idea. Step-father Deaf returns to station wagon blue with a paper bag brown.

I DID NOT LIKE THE LOOK IN HIS EYES OR THE WAY HIS BODY MOVED. THIS IS NOT GOOD. WHAT DID HE HAVE IN THE BAG? YOU WILL HAVE TO WAIT LIKE I DID. BUT NOT FOR LONG. IT'S ONLY A MINUTES DRIVE. EXIT THE PARKING LOT AND DRIVE

Down the entrance long to the side of the store. Parked and turned off the engine as we sat facing a dumpster. This still didn't seem too dangerous. After all, it's only 3 o'clock in the afternoon and cars use this driveway to enter and exit the store.

Instinct told me not to ask what was in the bag, but I was going to find out anyways. "Go ahead" "Pick one." he says. I had to reach in as he held the bag. I felt 3 items that made no sense. Cool, hard yet slimy, and rubbery.

I wanted to choose none. I didn't choose any. I didn't take anything out of the bag paper brown. Now in situations like these I learned it was a lose-lose situation. Yet I refused to be the instrument of my own humiliation. My purity supreme in my heartland.

So Stepfather Deaf did the choosing. He raised the Catholicness of my jumper plaid maroon to thigh high level as if I were a common whore for the passing motorists. "I must break you." He signed before reaching in the bag brown.

He chooses one and pulls it out. Who knew groceries were such dangerous items. I recognized a cucumber with what I now know to be a condom on it's tip. I do not remember much else until the cucumber with condom still attached was tossed with a piece of my soul into the bottom of the dumpster. With a deep part of me safe in a maroon plaid square, I wondered what would be done with the other two remaining offensive items. Would he be saving them for later?

HEARTLAND: THE PART OF A REGION CONSIDERED ESSENTIAL TO THE VIABILITY AND SURVIVAL OF THE WHOLE; ESPECIALLY A CENTRAL LAND RELATIVELY INVULNERABLE TO ATTACK. BY NOW, MY MAROON PLAID JUMPER HAS BEEN TRADED IN FOR A LOOSER PLAID MAROON SKIRT.

White shirt with Peter Pan collar and matching conservative maroon obligatory breast covering vest of seventh and eighth grade. I, for one, was grateful to be released from the restrictiveness of my maroon plaid jumper

And the extra added layer of protection from preying eyes I thought the vest afforded me. I thought as I grew older and into my new uniform, I would know what to do and how to stop the abuse in my life

But unlike my uniform
nothing had changed.
My days still dark.
No one to trust. Fear
my constant companion.
Adolescence compounds
my greasy shame.
New realities and worries
came with age and understanding. Being subjected to
awkward whole

CLASS TALKS ABOUT PRACTICING "GOOD PERSONAL HYGEINE" DAILY AND THE BIOLOGY of THE SPERM AND THE EGG FILMS... WHEN NUNS SEPERATED GIRLS AND BOYS into DIFFERENT CLASSES BECAUSE of too MUCH GIGGLING. THE WORDS of MY MOTHER HANGING THICK IN THE BATHROOM

Air as I placed my first sanitary napkin in my underwear. "Now you can get pregnant," feeling her underlying anger at me and the indignation I felt when she later said "You will be pregnant by the time you are 16." I knew for certain now my

Mother deaf knew about the sexual abuse. I certainly did not ever leave the house to fool around with local boys. Armed with new knowledge, I set out not to get pregnant by the time I was sixteen. I increased my hidden before and after school

Smoking behind L'il Peach habit. Nicotine was habit forming and may affect fertility according to the label on the side of the box. Other benefits menthol Kools provided included making my aloofness and lack of socializing with peers less noticeable and provided cover for me to be accepted by the "cool kids." I did acquire a pack and a half habit a day by the age of 16. Please don't think this strategy worked because I had no baby. I employed many different strategies that I thought would work. Some were completely ludicrous, some I am not proud of and make me feel complicit. I remind myself not to censure myself... Some ludicrous methods included jumping up and down, wiping myself raw, pouring carbonated beverages on my genitals and

A NOT SO PROUD METHOD. THIS METHOD INCLUDED LEARNING, FORGIVE MY BLUNTNESS.. HOW BEST TO JERK HIM OFF. TO ME JERKING HIM OFF FAST MEANT THERE WAS LESS CHANCE OF BEING MORE INTERNALLY VIOLATED. THE LESSER OF TWO EVILS

WHEN GIVEN NO CHOICE. THERE WAS ALSO the tried AND true MetHOD that HAD to Be USED ONLY SPARINGLY, SAVED FOR the OCCASIONS WHEN I COULD TAKE NO MORE. MY EARS, THE LOOKOUT ON NIGHTS STEP-FATHER DEAF WOKE ME FROM MY BED, tOLD

Him "Someone is awake" "Someone is coming." I used his deafness against him. the house quiet. The threat of discovery causing his desire to go limp. other days, I added days onto my period. Wearing a pad when I didn't bleed. I learned he didn't touch me at this time. if he didn't discover my period that month, I chose another week to wear pads. his hand on my ass feeling for a pad surprised me many a time. this strategy served me well throughout my days of the skirt maroon plaid and into my new public high school. Access to me while in my new high school presented some logistical challenges due to busing and integrating schools. The bus pick-up and drop-off inconvenient for step-father Deaf. He stepped it up taking me on more of those

DREADED out of town trips. OVERNIGHT STAYS IN MOTELS DID NOT AFFORD ME THE LUXURY of USING HIS DEAFNESS AGAINST HIM SINCE IT WAS JUST THE TWO OF US. I HAD to RETREAT INSIDE OF MYSELF AND ENDURE THE PRESSURE OF PREGNANCY, THE EVER MOUNTING levels of violence needed to satisfy step-father deaf's deeds, the growing anger at my mother's inaction, the world's blaring complacency, the utter isolation, desperation and despair and the sheer lack of trust in the world was causing me to fail in school. I "wasn't living up to my full potential." My step-father Deaf's growing threats to take me far away from home loomed large. I saw money as my only way out. The twins deaf were a problem but I thought I'd deal with that later.

After only present 52 days in Sub-Sophomore year and 3 days Sub Junior, I got my first job and quit High School. No one said or did much of anything. I earned $120.00 a week, then my mother deaf wanted $100.00 a week.

Now one might think I had a little freedom because I had a job but no, there were no trips to the movies, school dances, proms, first kisses or first dates. I worked and came straight home. My job a coffee shop two doors down from home.

I took orders from the customers keeping the conversations to a minimum. Stepfather Deaf developed a taste for coffee coming 4-5-6 times during my shifts to monitor my interactions. He would ingratiate himself with my co-workers using me as his interpreter box presenting himself through my words-tone-slant. once again my silence adds to my sense of complicity. the money I earned was divided with $100.00 going to mother deaf. the remaining $20. would go to me it would seem. my step-father deaf made a small wooden lockbox to "keep things safe." "Here's a key." "I will keep the other." "This is our runaway money." "Together." Naturally, I wasn't going to save money to allow more access. That plan was kaput. I didn't really know what to do even if I did have some money. What would I do about sisters twins?

I couldn't run away. What could I do? Once again, I was stuck. I got my G.E.D. I had decided that I could do nothing until I had a plan, but that looked more and more hopeless. Pressure within the home growing along with my blacksheep status. Step-father deaf threatening to take me away from my family loomed large. I didn't know at the time but my mother deaf was going to have baby number seven. My mother deaf's hostility towards me grew along with her belly. Stepfather Deaf decides to get out of Dodge for a while taking me on yet

Another road trip out of state to visit his family supposedly. While on the road, he leans over to expose my breasts to passing truckers. I don't remember much else at this time except that I felt my life constantly at risk. Now is most likely a good time to explain

DISSOCIATION. THIS IS A MENTAL PROCESS SOMEONE USES TO STAY SANE IN AN INSANE OR TRAUMATIC ENVIRONMENT. A COPING MECHANISM TO TURN OFF THE FEELINGS IF YOU CAN'T ESCAPE THE SITUATION. THIS IS PROBABLY THE

Reason I don't have too many specific memories of this time. Baby number seven last girl hearing was born somewhere within this time frame. My mother deaf was informed of step-father deaf's sexual abuse within the home but not by me. She could no longer feign ignorance. Armed with this info, my mother deaf decided to shift responsibility onto my shoulders. She labeled me "the other woman." She in her angry body of accusations did not make me feel safe enough to tell her. My heart and head knew

All along she had known for years yet turned a blind eye, as I had seen with my neighbor. She would fail to protect me. She blamed me. What would step-father deaf's consequence be? What if I told her and she continued to allow my stepfather deaf to live in the house? I decided based on what I knew. The best option for me was for me to keep my mouth shut and see what she'd do with the knowledge she had been given. Taking a wait and see approach had seemed my safest option.

Snippets from some Get out of Dodge ASL Road Trips.

Birds sleeping Crickets chirping
Moon beaming Wheel steering
Child drugging Barn waiting
Trouble looming Breath holding
Pulse racing Pulley squeaking
Hook busting Noose hanging
Rope burning Foot sleeping
Toes numbing Scalp burning

Fingers grazing Heartbeat thumping
Blood rushing Stomach churning
Abs twisting Lids squeezing
Muscles aching Mind closing
Sounds scaring Skin chafing
Emotions splitting Terror nearing
Eye peeking Acts depraving
Body thrashing Straps binding
Terror thriving Painful writhing
Body memorizing Heart hating

form menacing form messy
metal glinting brain screaming
image fleeting mind reeling
scissors snipping
bandsaw cutting
bucket dripping
buttocks shining disbelieving
hay itching evil grinning
semen squirting child raping
eyes rolling skin recoiling
time stopping moment freezing

Him Molesting   Self Frozen
Soul Mourning   Touch Repulsing
Bees Buzzing   Sun Rising
Ding-Dong Eating   Willow Weeping
Secret   Keeping
Mind   Doubting
Pen Writing   Hurried Describing
Body Hiding   Tree Telling
Tears   Flowing
Fingers   Cramping

thoughts rising forced forgetting
self protecting go on living
dirt digging paper folding
plastic wrapping secret hiding
no one finding soil covering
rain pelting roots tangling
time passing earth decaying
I like to believe that
weeping willow trees contain
salicylic acid in their tree
bark to ease a teller's pain.

Notes from a Civil Suit

When plaintiff was approximately sixteen her mother was informed by one of the children about on-going sexual abuse within the home. The mother then ordered defendant to leave the household. The defendant determined to continue the illicit behavior threatened to take the plaintiff away with him if she did not give the defendant a key to the house. When the mother discovered that plaintiff had given defendant a key, she ordered both defendant and plaintiff to move out of the house. This was in March 1986 when

Plaintiff was then 17 years old. Plaintiff then moved into a basement apartment of a co-worker and shortly thereafter in a matter of days the defendant joined her. I didn't see my family again for several years. The basement apartment consisted of a living and kitchen combo with shared laundry and one private bedroom. Once again I felt betrayed by those who should have known but didn't. After September of the same year, I got a different job, no longer employed with this co-worker woman hearing.

Notes from a Civil Suit
After November 1987 the
Defendant and Plaintiff
moved from the Basement
to a more Secluded House.
During this entire Period
Defendant had Sex with
the Plaintiff who had Become
Conditioned to Accept it as a
way of life. This continued

Until 1990 when plaintiff was twenty-two years old. There was no distractions or using the someone is coming strategy. It was just me and step-father. Deaf. Alone. Everyday. Me serving as his cook, maid, laundress, among other things. My life as tightly controlled as before. No contact with the outside world other than at work and with him. No dates with boys. No girlie chats on the phone. I went to work and straight home. 3:30 my expected arrival time. Not a minute later. Trips to the grocery store by myself came with a price. Having to leave a

Note with a detailed account of my whereabouts, task, expected arrival time, time of departure, and worst of all it must be signed with a declaration of love. Money always had to be accounted for. No chance for freedom. No place to go. Three years later, I saw an out. I learned I may not have to live this way any longer. I just needed a taste of freedom of how life could be. My step-father deaf

Still worked evenings. I believe this may have worked in my favor in allowing me to accept a job promotion. At the time, my job afforded me the opportunity to stay overnights at a residential facility. These two nights

A week enabled me to experience my own space for the first time in my life. To feel safe in my own bed. For many reasons, I cannot share a lot of particular detail around this specific time but can say I met some people that later had either a positive impact, negative impact, or both on my later life. I felt my situation at home becoming more dire. Perhaps step-father Deaf could sense a change in me. I was becoming aware that there was another way to live and that my life did not have to be this way. I snuck a copy of the book The Courage to Heal by Laura Davis and Ellen Bass into the house. I read it cover to cover in one night while step-father Deaf worked the overnight shift.

The topic of sexual abuse seemed to be everywhere now. It was on the news, in documentaries and on Oprah's talk show. My isolation had a crack of light finally. I was not the only one anymore.

Stepfather Deaf began talk of me quitting my job taking with it my only source of temporary refuge. He talked of impregnating me. I knew I must not get pregnant at all costs. I cared more for a non-existent being than I did for myself at the time. I had been so badly mistreated, abandoned, and unloved. I was not going to provide step-father Deaf an opportunity to hurt someone else. My thoughts were to either kill myself or overcome insurmountable fear of leaving and being killed by him. I had to overcome this fear somehow and take my chances. There was fear of the unknown. I would have to hide. Very well.

WHERE DO I GO? I DID NOT THINK OF MYSELF AS A CHILD ANYMORE AND I THOUGHT I WASN'T ELIGIBLE TO CALL 1-800-4-A-CHILD. I DIDN'T THINK OF MYSELF AS A BATTERED WOMAN ELIGIBLE FOR A SHELTER. I DID NOT DRIVE. I DIDN'T KNOW

How to navigate around town outside of my go straight there and come straight back existence. I had no friends, family, or money. I had no safe place. My job and refuge in jeopardy. I thought hard about who could

Help me. Who could I tell? Could I even get the words out? Would this be the time step-father Deaf announced he could really hear after all this time? He played so many mind games all the time.

Step-father deaf went to work that night. I sat myself in the bathroom. Deciding. Do I die here in the bathroom? Medicine cabinet full. No one to find me until morning. I could not subject another

Human being to this life. I thought about my drowning experience and all that had been told to me. This was not the way out. For a long time I just sat in the bathroom. There was no one I trusted. So I wrote a letter to God.

A letter to God who had let me down numerous times before. A God who hung on my bedroom wall watching me from his wooden cross. A God who my mother deaf told me was seeing me "lie all the time."

My "Black-Hearted" Self. A God who watched as I slept in the Jesus Christ position. God who spit me back up from the cold, salty sea. My letter to God was intercepted at work the next day. Wheels set in motion

Without too much detail, I explained to my co-worker who had snatched my letter to God that I needed out of my living situation. Together we hatched a plan for getting out at the end of the school term.

I would get out but the go where question remained. I would have to worry about that later. The first priority was to make it out of the house alive and get away. It was a long few weeks. The date carefully chosen.

June 15th 1990. That day was a Friday. Graduation day. A half-a-school day followed by a week's vacation. A rarity. This half-day would, unbeknownst to step-father Deaf, enable me a three hour head start on my get-away plan. I still didn't know where I would go, but at this point it didn't matter. If I stayed, I would not be allowed to continue working after vacation, and I'd be condemned I felt to a life of hell.

Thursday June 14th was the last hellish day I would spend in the home. That afternoon, I would begin my back-to-back shift, complete with overnight stay at my job site.

I spent all Thursday knowing that this was a most dangerous time. I was filled with dread that at any moment step-father Deaf could show up unannounced at my job to thwart my attempt at freedom. Permanently. When I left home on Thursday, I felt I had no choice but to take $50.00 from the lockbox containing $1700.00 without a written accounting. This $50.00 would have to get me through the week until my next paycheck somehow. A paycheck that, for once, would be all mine. I was worried my actions would give me away. I remembered my first and only attempt at trying

to take money unnoticed.
I had discovered a clerical
error in the cashbox
ledger. I wasn't sure
if step-father Deaf
was aware of the amount
in the moneybox since
he pretended never to
know how much was
in there and that

He never unlocked it. I thought maybe with the clerical error, I could begin an escape fund. I left the house with the money leaving the required note complete with destination and expected departure and arrival time since he was sleeping from his overnight shift. I headed to the mall that had a bank. Gone just under an hour, I returned to a still sleeping stepfather Deaf. I thought my plan a big success. I thought wrong. Stepfather Deaf rose from his supposed slumber and questioned my whereabouts. I told the truth about going to the mall, but lied about the bank. He then asked me about putting the specific dollar amount in the bank. I knew then he had set a trap for me. Had he diabolically followed me in his car? Pretended to be asleep? How often did he really check the cash lockbox he pretended never to touch? As a punishment for taking money, I was to "give me a good one." That meant a very bad sexual trauma would be occurring for me. Step-father deaf was always setting traps and playing mind games to try to get me to "break the rules" so he could punish me saying I "owed him a good one." At times, I wondered if he was really even deaf.

I never took money again. Until June 14th that is. Thursday June 14th was the last official morning I would spend in the Home. Everything hinged on successfully leaving that day. That evening I would begin my back-to-

Back shift with the overnight stay. I spent all day Thursday and all day Friday worried and fearful with the knowledge that stepfather Dear could, at any moment, show up at my job thwarting my attempt at freedom.

permanently. He could arrive unannounced and due to the language barrier, threaten me right in front of others. I wasn't sure if my demeanor had given me away as I hid my nervousness. I carefully considered

Whether it would be wise to take any of the money contained in the lockbox. I decided that I had no choice to risk taking $50.00 from the lockbox. This money would have to last me until my next paycheck. A paycheck that would for the first time be mine. I took it without a written accounting figuring I'd make up some excuse if I got caught. With nowhere to stay, I knew at least I could buy some food. It would not be large enough a sum to raise suspicion, but would most definitely rise to the level of a "give me a good one" punishment. Hopefully, I would not be seeing the twist in his body, his hooded lids and his leering mouth with the slightest hint of a smile as he signed this to me. Ever again.

Words from a Collage

Courage garnered up.
Trying not to swallow hard.
Mentally reviewing plans.
Reassuring myself.
One hour to freedom.
I watch the clock.
Tick-tock tick-tock.
Don't arouse suspicion.
Look at something else.

I discard laundry on
top of a pile. His
smells. His stains.
They will remain unwashed.
I smile to myself.
45 minutes to freedom
I watch the clock.
I look around. Regretfully,
I must leave behind
my Raggedy Ann doll

The keeper of pain. I say goodbye to that I will not miss. The known for the unknown. Goodbye to dingy old confining walls. All the evil aged yellow. 30 minutes to freedom. I watch the clock.

tick-tock tick-tock. Survival depends on my success today. I can take no more. Eyes watchful. Ears straining. Breath stilled. Heart wildly thumping. 15 minutes to freedom. I watch the clock.

tick-tock tick-tock. It's now or never. I swallow my stomach. Minutes stretching into hours. Agony. Money, a pebble in my shoe. Calm down. Try to breathe normally. My survival hidden in my underwear. It itches.

Act like it's just another day I tell myself.
Minutes to freedom.
The time ticks near.
My cell door creaks open, breaking years of busted metal—painstakingly slow.
My taste of freedom increases as does my fear.

I AM traveling into the unknown. My bus toward freedom encroaches. I wait without breathing. I pay my fare. I step onto the bus bravely afraid and so begins my life.

BiG LeAP

I made the leap. Overcoming my fear. This was a very dangerous task. I went to work. I watched and waited. I wondered. Had step-father Deaf discovered the missing money? Would he come to my job and thwart my last shot at freedom? I would have to wait some more. I was not out of the woods yet. I remember nothing else of that night. Don't know if I slept. Probably not.

It's morning again. Happy graduation day. Only 5 more hours to go. I mentally reassured myself that step-father deaf would have been here by now had he been very concerned with the amount of missing

Money. I thought I chose the right amount. Not enough to ring any alarm bells, but most definitely a "give me a good one" amount. Noon time. Pomp and Circumstance plays. Finally. Time to go. Anywhere

But here, a three-hour headstart from the time I was expected to be home. No exceptions. I cannot give details about leaving. All I can remember is leaving in terror. Drive! Go! Hurry! My co-worker

MAN HEARING WHO INTERCEPTED MY LETTER TO GOD WAS DRIVING. DRIVE. GO. AWAY FROM THE CITY. IT IS SAID THE MOST DANGEROUS TIME FOR AN ABUSED PERSON IS WHEN THEY ARE TRYING TO LEAVE. I BELIEVE THAT.

As we drove around, I saw the city I had never been allowed to see. I had no idea where I was, but was taken to a house where I was asked to make some phone calls to alert others I was

Okay. I made three phone calls. One to co-worker female. She knew nothing of my home life. But was the primary person I worked my shifts with day-in and day-out. My step-father deaf was aware of who I worked my shifts with and when. It was my belief he would surely contact her to try and find me. I was correct. I did not tell her my shameful secret. The perception was that I had run off with a boy, leaving

A POOR, DISTRAUGHT, WORRIED, DEAF, HELPLESS, UNABLE to COMMUNICATE WITH THE WORLD, STEPFATHER BEHIND. ME AN UNCARING, SELFISH, MEAN DAUGHTER. NATURALLY, ANYONE WOULD WANT to HELP THIS MAN LOCATE HIS WAYWARD DAUGHTER.

Well aware of this fact, I did not tell co-worker female of my whereabouts. Only that I left of my own volition. The first surprising thing I learned was step-father deaf had brazenly involved the police to help him search, confident fully in my silence. They were looking for me. The second surprising yet-not-surprising thing was this poor, pathetic step-father deaf manipulated police into searching for a grown 22 year old

WOMAN MISSING 1-3 HOURS, DEPENDING ON WHETHER ONE FACTORS IN THE RARE HALF-WORK DAY. WHATEVER HAPPENED TO THE MISSING 24 HOUR RULE? STEP-FATHER DEAF ALWAYS PLAYED UPON THE SYMPATHY OF OTHERS,

including the police.
I had seen it before.
Avoiding well-deserved
traffic tickets. Police
who tapped steamed
up windows of station
wagon blue with
flashlights in the
darkness of night.
Illegally parked behind

the side of the road
and in lover's lanes.
Me, still in my jumper
plaid maroon, interpreting
the words "get moving"
"get on your way"
or "you can't park
here" while my head
screams "deaf people
can't talk in the dark

You idiot!" My second call was to step-father Deaf. Mostly to get him off everyone's back. I did not want to call, but did so at co-workers urging. The only things I remember about this conversation was I was not coming home and telling step-father deaf what he did to me was not love in response to his "I love yous." I ended the conversation knowing he was still a threat to me and he would not give up looking for me. My third call was to the police. I told them I was fine, not missing, hadn't been taken and that I would not be going home again. In order to clear their file, they needed me to come down in person to the Police Station. No way. I had gotten away cleanly, and I was going to stay hidden for the time being. Unbeknownst to me, step-father Deaf had shown up at a co-worker's home asking questions. With good intentions,

Co-worker hearing tried to arrange a meeting with myself and her in an attempt to reconcile step-father deaf with me. I refused to meet with her. Her mother's sage advice was "Not everything may be as it seems" stopped

Stepfather Deaf's further visits to her home. I later learned he parked at the end of her dead-end street, with the hope of locating me. Lie in wait: for someone or something to stay hidden, waiting for someone or something.

I would remain a missing person. No way was I going to set foot in that town. It is not known how stepfather Deaf learned co-worker's address. I did not know it. It is another glaring example of manipulation. The only ones thought to have given out the address would have been the police, my employer, or worse yet, step-father Deaf had followed her. A frightening thought. I do not remember the circumstances surrounding the two kind women of

Putnam who took me, a stranger, into their home that evening and subsequently let me stay the week as well. I suspect they were members of a local church. I was eternally grateful, yet feared for their safety.

Knowing this housing was only temporary, I attempted to make my return to work in a weeks time a little bit safer. I obtained a restraining order through the local court. It was here that I was put in touch with the District Attorney's office and started a lengthy 2 year court process to criminally prosecute step-father Deaf for some of his crimes. While staying with the kind Putnam women, co-worker male escorted me to the Police Station armed with a restraining order. Together, the Police and I served notice to stepfather Deaf at his job. They then accompanied me to the house while I gathered more of my personal belongings. While

At the house I looked for some specific pieces of evidence. One: A black revolver. Two: An "I must break you!" rubber dildo wrapped in crumpled tinfoil kept in the bedside table drawer. Three: A mountain of crumpled up semen-stained tissues discarded between the mattress and the wall. All of these things had been taken out of the house and cleaned up. Step-father Deaf must not have been as comfortable or confident in my

Silence after the visit from the police for he reportedly made an out-of-state roadtrip to purchase a rifle. He was spotted by a neighbor removing it from the trunk of his car. I imagine it was especially for me.

Armed with a restraining order and my temporary housing coming to an end, I set out about the business of securing a live-in position at my job. What choice did I have? I still ran the risk of step-father Deaf coming to my job.

I HAD NO CHOICE But to Rely on that court-ordered piece of paper until a better option came along. I lived in terror, but it WASN'T ANY WORSE THAN WHAT I ALREADY LIVED THROUGH. Looking back, it probably helped that I was a bit numbed to everything. If Step-father Deaf showed up, it would not be to take me home, but to commit an act of violence. I rarely left my protective walls at that time. I traded one prison for a better one. Step-father Deaf must have gotten wind that I was looking to prosecute as he fled the state soon afterwards. I participated in numerous interviews, videotaping, discussed jurisdictional issues, and had to open myself and reveal the most painful and embarassing stuff. Each day left me a collapsed heap of tired.

I testified at Grand Jury, talking to all kinds of strangers about the most intimate and very personal details of my malnourished life. 60 indictments were then handed down by the Grand Jury. The District Attorney was not hopeful we would go to trial

Since Step-father Deaf fled the state and the "Commonwealth does not have the funds to search for this guy." This would mean Step-father Deaf getting away again with what he had done his whole life, and would most likely do again to some poor disadvantaged woman with children. I was determined to try to do for others what no one did for me. That meant finding him. One Columbus Day weekend, co-worker male friend and me took a much different out-of-state roadtrip.

The Commonwealth would ask the local police to arrest him if we had a physical address for step-father Deaf. Co-worker Hearing and I set out to try and locate his new address, and we did just that.

This very familiar ride was different this time. There was no sudden groping or exposing my breasts to passing truckers. When I spoke to co-worker recently, he reminded me of details I had forgotten. Being a

Holiday weekend and peak foliage season, hotels were fully booked. We slept in the car outside a Seven-Eleven. It is like tunnel vision for me and my memory. The only thing I can remember is being in both homes of

Step-father Deaf's siblings. First sister hearing, then brother hearing. Both were given a brief overview of Step-father Deaf's behavior over the years. They denied any prior knowledge, but both said they were "not surprised" and shared a bit of their own history.

They both gave me step-father Deaf's new address and did not put up their homes as bail. This was the extent of the support I got from them, and they never spoke to me again. Upon my arrival home, I gave the address to the

Authorities. I do not know what happened on Step-father Deaf's end. Did his sister and brother tell him of my visit? My best guess is "No," because a few weeks later on Halloween night, I received a message on my answering machine telling me that he had finally been arrested. Step-father Deaf waived his extradition rights and was flown back to the Commonwealth in the company of authorities. I was not required to attend the arraignment, but I chose to come anyway. An arraignment is the first appearance an arrested person makes in court, which is the next business day after one's arrest. At the arraignment, the criminal

CHARGES ARE OFFICIALLY READ OUT LOUD IN COURT. MOST PEOPLE PLEAD "NOT GUILTY" AT THIS POINT. I HAD NOT SEEN STEP-FATHER DEAF IN ABOUT SIX MONTHS. I DID NOT WANT TO MISS HIS ARREST. I REMEMBER SITTING IN THE BACK OF THE COURT-

Room feeling sick at the enormity of it all. When the court officer called step-father Deaf's name, my body left me and floated up to the ceiling as I watched his 220LB. frame fill the doorway into court.

His appearance, dirty and disheveled. Hands shackled behind his back in handcuffs awkwardly pleading. I notice his missing dentures - the ones kept for years in a glass by the sink. I notice

His bright orange sweatshirt with a black-stained beer belly. His grime-stiffened blue jeans. He is as I remember. From the back row, I smell oily never washed hair. Nicotined

Rough fat fingertips yellowed half-inch thick nails on his sausage fingers. All seven of them. Fingers that at one time told me that I might suffer the same mysterious fate. I survived my ordeal - all ten fingers intact.

I notice the same workboots brown with the heavy steel toes. The boots that thud and then thud as step-father deaf goes to bed before work. I listen cautiously for what might come next. An approximation of the "SH" sound that meant I was being summoned to the bedroom. The "Doctor Who" theme song echoes in my head as I wish for my very own tardis to teleport me anywhere but here. "You must

"Help me sleep," he'd say. I'd return to catch the end of "Doctor Who." Usually. But not always. Rarely allowed in my mother's bedroom, I wait for three clicks of the hurricane lamp. In the light, I search for and never find

Ah, Jesus Christ peephole as I stare over stepfather Deaf's bare white shoulders and squared tense sweaty buttocks. "Not guilty" my stepfather Deaf says through the mouth of his court-appointed public defender.

His own mouth contorted.
The face usually made
when he lied. Bail
was set. He was taken
away still in handcuffs.
Thoughts like he could
get out filled my head.
All kinds of what ifs?
I nod woodenly as

The District Attorney tells me that I will be notified if he makes bail, all the while thinking the justice system has it wrong letting this man out. But it appears the accused have many more rights.

It was some time before I felt comfortable believing no one, not even his siblings, were going to bail him out of jail. He would be remaining in jail until trial. Waiting for trial is not like you see on television. There are

Hearings and delays. Everything I told the district attorney is shared with the defense. The trial does not start with bruises still fresh on the victim's face. Wheels of justice grind slowly. It was over a year when the trial began. Step-father deaf sat in jail all that time. At the same time, I had to begin to heal my life and deal with my abuse and its aftermath. Everyone's journey is different. There is no set roadmap to follow.

I wish there were some easy instruction manual that one could check off boxes on a master-to-do list. I just had to go with it. Step-father Deaf had stolen my past. He could not have my future.

I had to venture out into the world and learn life. Leave the safety of my walls. Go out. Step-father deaf in jail. I had to learn practical things. Open accounts. Pay bills. Write a check. Embarassing things most twenty-two year olds would know. I had to be interacting and talking with people and the general public in my own voice. I had to learn how to navigate the city. How to use public transportation. Go places I had never been.

do things I had never done. I had to learn about choices and what was out there in the world. I was no longer living my come-straight-home-from-school-and-work existence. I had to learn to make choices for myself and only myself. I had to push through panic and guilt, learn that this was okay to do for myself. There would only be my own consequences, not a "you must give me a good one" if I wanted something. The first place I decided to go to by myself was the local mall. I hadn't been there, but I knew it was only a straight shot 10 minute walk down the street. No confusing turns, and as I walked, the intended

Goal of the mall would be within my eyesight. Once there, I realized I did not have a practical reason for being there. So I sat in the busy food court to think. Sbarro Taco Burger King Japanese Coke Pepsi Sprite Pizza Noodles

Burgers fries large small plain cheese pepperoni sausage vegetable teriyaki on and on and on. There were too many choices. For once, it was up to me what to eat. It was overwhelming. No. I was not hungry.

There were people, sound, colors, choices, neon signs everywhere. I was beginning to see the world in color as if I had been in a semi-coma for my whole life and I was waking up. I look around some more. There

Are books, music, and clothing stores of interest. Should I try the music store? I feel guilty about that and would not know what to get. I don't know any artists or what I'd like. I think about not wanting to waste my own money for the first time on something

Stupid. Maybe a clothing store would be a better choice? What store do I choose? What kind of clothes should I buy? Shirts, pants, shoes? I think about how I can buy any clothes I want now. I don't know what colors I like.

I think about the fact that I don't have to choose clothing with protection in mind. I don't have to think about how unsexy, unappealing, or drab it should be. I don't have to look for clothes that I think will

hinder easy access. I
look at all the people
hustling about chatting
carrying different bags
and waiting in lines
at the food court.
All these people making
decisions with ease.
All the colors intense.
I realize I had lived

My entire life as if in a dark gloomy grey fog. Too many things I had missed out on. Then I had a panic attack. I had yet to experience myself as my own seperate person. A person seperate from the words, needs, wants and among other things, the opinion of others.

I had to learn my own likes, dislikes, thoughts, and feelings about things. My parents deaf had squashed all expression, qualities in me, and emotions that did not match their own. I had learned long ago to keep watchful and very silent.

My thoughts and feelings protected by being squashed down and secret. I had been abandoned in many countless ways over and over again. I had to recover that self. I had virtually brought up my own self, all the while receiving negative messages my entire life. Never positive. To heal from this was going to take some doing. Realization hits that being free is not going to be enough. Therapy. There I said it. Support groups. Trusting another person. Using my own voice. Telling. Being heard finally. Risking. I was going to have to have help sifting through years of anger, grief, guilt, shame, and loss. The healing process is a lifetime journey of learning how to work through each layer of pain to become a functional, thriving adult. In childhood, my natural progression of developmental steps were derailed by sexual abuse. I had to come to terms with the fact that as an adult, I was not going to get what I needed or missed as a child. No one could make up for my childhood losses. Ever. I had to mourn what I didn't get as a child. Getting in touch with feelings and being present in my body was going to be a painful process. But as I healed, my capacity to sit with and tolerate my feelings would improve. I needed to learn how to take care of myself by

Learning to set limits, have good boundaries, and by silencing and opposing inner critics. By using kind and gentle language with myself and by always acknowledging the silenced parts of myself. I had to nurture my strengths, and soothe myself when experiencing intense grief, anxiety, and depression. All of us on this healing journey must learn to know and face our

Horrible truths. We need to stop doubting and questioning ourselves and our memories partial or complete. We must confront our own denial and minimization of our experiences and eventually look in the face of WHAT IS. We MUST HAVE courage in a family or society that MAY Not WISH to ACKNOWLEDGE that SEXUAL PREDATORS ARE iN OUR MIDST.

the decisions. The decisions of others to choose denial over truth adds another degree of suffering on what is already an incredibly lonely journey. We must learn how to break free of old patterns that trap us in the circumstances that repeat past injuries. We must learn to remove ourselves from unhealthy relationships, situations, or thought patterns that keep us from

Moving from victim to survivor. It is important to have compassion for ourselves. That any positive step that is taken on one day is not erased if it isn't taken on the next. Each step has cumulative value.

I had to get past crippling shame and feelings of violation, humiliation, and helplessness that were a result of sexual abuse. Healing shame meant ridding myself of my own feelings of

Self-judgement, inadequacy, worthlessness, self-loathing, and fear of rejection that like an undercurrent, pulls one into a downward spiral. I must give a voice to the silenced, disowned parts of myself that feel the stigma of my differentness. I had to identify the origin of my shame right at the roots and place it at the feet of where it truly belonged. The blame lies with the people who failed to protect me time and time again. But most of all at the people who made the choice to perpetrate pure evil. I had to shake loose the beliefs and attitudes that shackled me to the perpetrators and lay the blame fully at their feet.

"All Rise." Says the court officer. "Do you solemnly and sincerely declare and affirm that the evidence you shall give will be the truth, the whole truth, and nothing but the truth?"

"I do," I replied as I returned to my body. What was expected to be a three day trial turned into a two week trial with me on the witness stand for three harrowing days. Step-father Deaf

Also took the stand lying through the mouth of the certified interpreter. It's jury deliberation day. They file back into the courtroom three more times to ask the judge for clarification on the jury instructions.

The jurors wanted further instructions on the meaning of reasonable inference. We will never know what questions or discussions were in the mind of the jury while in deliberation. The judge gave his final example to the jurors about the meaning of reasonable inference. His example was if one leaves the house in the morning and there is no mail and you return home after work and there is mail, one can reasonably believe the mailman came by.

The jurors exit the courtroom single file to further deliberate. Not for long though. The jury verdict is in. They file back in, their faces unreadable. They looked at neither me nor step-father Deaf. A pure agonizing wait

As they each one by one take their seats in the jury box. The court officer reads the charges and asks if the jury has reached a verdict. The jury nods. The judge asks for the verdict. "Not Guilty," answers the jury foreman.

"Not Guilty" reverberates in my head as each of the jury members are polled individually. They are mistaken, I silently scream. I tantrum and vow silently that I will never get up from this hard wooden creaky courtroom bench until I felt justice was served. These twelve people were just like the others who failed to act. Another part of society who underreacted to events in my life.

Like the physician who passed the burden of my malnourished life onto others, the teachers who pretended not to see the marks on my body, the teachers who questioned the marks and still did not do something. Neighbors who lived next door, who asked why I never played outside, who then closed their own doors pretending not to see. Relatives who lived above me who asked "what was all that racket last night?"

the racket of being
beaten awake, dragged
from my bed and
bounced off walls.
Relatives who shut
both their eyes and
ears and mouths
thereafter. The priest
who told me after
confessing to not

following the commandment
to honor my mother
and father that this
"was God's plan for me."
Dentists and doctors.
Shoppers who parked
their cars next to
ours in parking lots
at the mall in the hot
summer sun who had

Returned hours later only to find me still sitting there in a baking car. Their arms laden with bags unlocking their cars and driving away. The court system who ignored biological father

Deaf's allegations of sexual abuse based on his physical appearance and less-than-stellar criminal record. The policeman who tapped on fogged-up windows of station wagon blue and drove away. The jurors were like

the passing motorists
and truckers on the
out-of-town roadtrips
south who sped up
for a second look.
Not for a license
plate or description,
but a better look at
my exposed breast.

sleazy motel and hotel operators who looked on blankly while checking us in for the night, teachers who stated over and over again that I "was not living up to my potential" as they

Were the ones who failed to report 52 days absent one year and 177 days absent the next. But most of all, like my mother deaf, these jurors knew. I had spoken my truth in that room for three days.

Not guilty, times twelve. One juror, not three feet from me, I could see the pain in his eyes as I testified. Not guilty. The courtroom empties. People are also milling about. I am alone with my thoughts.

Step-father Deaf is now a free man. How can I be safe? What will happen next? Will he come after me? I can't leave the bench. How could the jurors have done this? How could they not believe me? Did they like so

MANY others, excuse step father Deaf's behavior out of sympathy for his deafness? He seemed to think so or was it about not wanting to think heinous things happen to children? The jurors must have seen me rooted to my seat as they exited the room one after another. The jurors wanted to get a message to me so they asked the District Attorney to deliver another slap in the face. They wanted me to know that they believed me. Believed me! Yet, did not convict. Knew and did nothing.

It was difficult or next to impossible to try and reason why they reached the verdict they did. Would it have been better for me to not know they believed me? I saw one of the jurors a few months later.

the one who sat 3 feet from me. I could not get off the bus fast enough to catch him so I will never know. Yes, I had pried myself off the courtroom bench only with the help of a supportive friend hearing and the unwillingness of giving a grinning stepfather deaf the satisfaction of seeing me in distress. Logic tells me the jurors felt there was not enough evidence for conviction. Short of PREGNANCY AND SEXUALLY TRANSMITTED DISEASE, RARELY IS there evidence of sexual assault. Predators fear physical force will make the child tell. Sexual predators like step-father Deaf engage in a more gradual calculated process. They work stealthily honing in on vulnerabilities and lack of social supports.

Step-father Deaf with methodical cunning, sought ways to exploit the emotional void in my life created by my mother Deaf. Step-father Deaf worked with catlike precision to gain my trust and respect pretending to care about my feelings and validate how awfully Mother Deaf was treating me, and making me believe he was just as helpless in stopping it. It is only now as an adult that I realize Stepfather Deaf did have power to stop Mother Deaf's torturous behavior and treatment of me. He, in fact

Had a hand in creating punishments that Mother deaf chose to carry out. He helped create and took advantage of my troubled relationship with Mother deaf and had established himself as someone with a sympathetic ear. No pun intended.

for his own selfish gain. He worked hard to create a false emotional connection that ultimately led to a massive betrayal of my trust. He deliberately set out to fill the emotional void in my life making me feel special or loved for the very first time in my life. He complimented me, stroked my hair, consoled me with hugs, introducing non-sexual touch never before received. He then introduced secrecy in bad mouthing my mother deaf's behavior and in his consoling words. Once I was emotionally invested in the relationship, stepfather Deaf with cunning precision, pushed the boundaries into more overt touching. Stepfather Deaf showered me with affection, compliments and hints of sexual desire. He was teaching me about "love." Given my confusion and lack of sexual knowledge, I was afraid to object and potentially lose the only "good" relationship in my life.

In doing so, step-father Deaf made me feel very complicit in feeling I had invited the sexual abuse. I blamed myself for this immense betrayal of trust and the lack of my own ability to foresee this situation. I took the

Responsibility for
this lack of judgement
and despite being a
child with limited
understanding, heaped
the responsibility
onto my own shoulders.
Perhaps it was years
of interpreting the world
and being the ears

of my parents that added to my burden. Shame increased as step-father deaf escalated his manipulations and sexual behaviors thereby securing my compliance. Setting up a scenario for repeated continual victimization and learned helplessness. This is what I wished the jury knew. These things leave no evidence... Lack of information. Lack of privacy. Leaving the door open in the bathroom. Being exposed to pornography, exposure to inappropriate nudity, uncomfortable hugs, fondling of genitals or breasts, penetration with a finger or object, sexual harassment, sexual interest, or the ogling of one's body and the list goes on and on. I never saw step-father Deaf again after the verdict, despite living with the threat of it daily. Perhaps step-father Deaf wisely heeded my threats to criminally prosecute him on other unfiled charges, in any number of other counties and states where crimes had been committed should he bother me again.

He died eight years later of pancreatic cancer. His career of molestation ended but not soon enough for me. His legacy of pain lives on and I live with the fallout on a daily basis. Now if you are anything like me you wanted to shut this book in disgust after the not guilty verdict. But despite the legal outcome, one of the most important steps for me was the process of finally breaking years of silence and shame and the taking back of my power. Breaking this silence had enabled me to take small steps toward rebuilding my life. Seeing and hearing reactions to my story, at the District Attorney's office and those who shared my outrage validated my experiences.

Speaking my truth allowed me to confront my abuser and choose truth over denial. In that courtroom, I no longer saw stepfather Deaf as big, looming and powerful, but as a weak crumpled pathetic liar who stole goodness from children unable to muster any of his own. I saw a man unable to have normal relationships with adults. An empty shell of a man with vacant eyes and a slackened mouth.

Now it's been some time since I spoke of my escape. I would like to remind you about co-worker male that fateful rainy night. My god letter folded and in a small square when co-worker male playfully snatched it from my hands. I don't know if I would have had the courage to show it to anyone but fate stepped in. A conversation ensued. Setting destiny and plans of escape from Step-father Deaf into motion.

My secret finally told. I shudder to think what may have happened otherwise. Step-father deaf threatening me to quit my job, my only shot to gain my freedom. The only option I felt I had at the time.

It was my only source of interaction with the outside world. My two night-a-week safe haven from sexual abuse. My first small taste of what life could be like on the outside of my isolating house walls. Nights I could sleep easier. Stepfather Deaf was also trying to impregnate me to trap me further and bring another life into the world of suffering, isolation and sexual abuse. I knew one way or another I could never be responsible for the suffering of another and the situation was becoming very dire for me. I was quickly coming to the end of my rope and what small hopes I had were dying more and more each day.

One spring evening, I begin the obligatory task of waking up stepfather Deaf for his evening 11p-7am shift. 10:10pm a dangerous time. I prayed for a difficult wake-up, one that would eat up the time on the clock so there would be no time for a "you owe me" kind of night. Step-father Deaf was difficult to wake, often falling back to sleep. Me, a human snooze button tapping and then shaking him as 11:00 PM approached. Finally he is awake and out the door without incident. This time confident he was gone, I went into the bathroom. I took a long look at myself. It was decision time. I could begin taking everything that was inside the mirror medicine cabinet. I had enough in there to be successful and I was confident I would remain undiscovered until 7:10 A.M. Another dangerous time. I resolved that I would not bring a life into this world to suffer and that I would be done with this life once and for all.

Murder was out of the question, suicide and Catholic teachings filled my head. Mother Dear's "God sees you" seared into my mind's eye. The eyes staring back at me knew this was not who I was and that I had fought too long and too hard to quit now. I thought about my life and the drowning experience I had as a young girl. The message that I had to return to life for a purpose. Another instance where I was told I wasn't living up to my potential.

How long was I to suffer this learning experience? What was there to possibly gain from this experience? I saw no way out now or then. I did not see any kind of solution at the time. I decided to give up in a different way.

THAT NIGHT IN THE BATHROOM
AND OVER THE COURSE OF
A FEW DAYS, I BEGAN
COMPOSING A GOD LETTER.
ADDRESS UNKNOWN. EACH
PAGE A SMALL FOLDED
SHAPE FLAT IN MY POCKET.
I WAS GIVING UP THE
PROBLEM. GIVING IT TO

God to solve. I didn't know I would be free in about a month's time. I always thought I should know what to do. But I shouldn't be hard on myself as I wasn't taught these skills

AS A CHILD AND WASN't GOING TO MAGICALLY KNOW THEM AS AN ADULT. IT HAS TAKEN ME A VERY LONG TIME TO REALLY KNOW THIS. TO REALLY BELIEVE AND KNOW THIS IN MY BONES.

Excerpt from a God Letter

Here I am. I hope you are listening. There are many times I felt you haven't heard me. I know I am just one person out of many and it may sound very selfish but I have wanted to be free for a very long time now. I do not know what your plan is for me. But I feel I have suffered enough. I don't have any more strength. I feel I can accomplish so much if I can only get past this. Why won't you help me? Maybe it's because

I don't have enough faith.
But I think I lost it
along the way. Maybe
even given up hope in a
just God. It's been just
about 20 years of agony.
I'm worried my life
will never be my own.
I'll probably never be free
But I can tell you I would

use my experience to my advantage and help others but I can't get myself out of this by myself. I need your help. I am sorry that I have lost faith but through my experiences it's hard to believe that I could go through all this and emerge unscathed. I wish

I could believe like a child can and see the world through young eyes. I can't even remember a time when I did. It's hard to believe there is so much evil and suffering in this world and yet such beauty like the rain I hear tonight washing the earth clean.

But in the morning when the rain stops evil remains and festers again. Please help take this problem away. Do it your way but do it soon. It may sound selfish but I would like my life to be mine for once. I promise to have good come from it.

AfteRWARD

Reasons kids don't tell. Children may be deprived of basic information about sexuality and may not realize what abusive behavior is or that it is wrong. They may equate goodness with obedience to adults. Sexual abuse is often presented as evidence of affection and children are confused about sexual misbehavior. Uninformed children trust all adults. Children feel powerless and may not know that they can say no to adults.

Children may have fears that no one will believe them. They may not have language to describe their experiences if abuse occurs very young. They are afraid of getting in trouble or being labeled bad. Kids may have been threatened physically, verbally and emotionally. Kids may have fears about losing family or people close to them. Children fear the abuser and the repercussions in telling. Children may not want to risk the family being split up. There are so many reasons children may have shame that they were betrayed by someone they trusted. They may feel guilty that despite this they may still love or care about the abuser. They may feel guilt or shame about sexual abuse occurring in the first place and that they couldn't stop it or tell anyone. They may feel shame or guilt for continuing secrecy and feel responsible for ongoing abuse. Children may feel shame about being very powerless to stop abuse. Now that we understand some of the many reasons children may not tell about being abused, here's what to do

If kids do tell, calmly listen. Believe the child. Reassure them it was not their fault. Don't blame them for doing or not doing something. Praise them for their immense bravery. Comfort them by reassuring them they did the right thing by trusting you enough to tell you. They may even be feeling very panicked right then and may even want to recant their story. Honor the trust that they gave you by protecting them. Do something. Take immediate action to maintain their safety. If the abuse was recent that means they need medical attention. Contact the police station or local child protection authorities. If you are unsure where these are in your state you can contact CHILDHELP A National Child Abuse Protection Hotline.

The number is 1-800-4-A-CHILD 1-800-442-4453. There is also www.childhelp.org Crisis counselors are on duty 24/7. All children need your protection. Those with special needs need us to be extra vigilant. You, please do your part.

www.ingramcontent.com/pod-product-compliance
Lightning Source LLC
Chambersburg PA
CBHW070549100426
42744CB00006B/248